CARDIFF'S
VANISHED DOCKLANDS

BRIAN LEE

The
History
Press

First published in 2006 by
Sutton Publishing

Reprinted 2007

Reprinted in 2010 by
The History Press
The Mill, Brimscombe Port,
Stroud, Gloucestershire, GL5 2QG
www.thehistorypress.co.uk

Title page photograph: Sacks of potatoes are
unloaded at Queens Dock, 1947.

All photographs courtesy of Associated
British Ports/Cardiff Council, unless
otherwise indicated.

British Library Cataloguing in Publication Data
A catalogue record for this book is available from the
British Library.

ISBN 978-0-7509-4424-3

Typeset in 10.5/13.5 Photina.
Typesetting and origination by
Sutton Publishing.
Printed and bound in Great Britain by
Marston Book Services Limited, Didcot

Butetown and Cardiff Docks is also available from The History Press

Dedicated to Frank Hennessy,
the true son of the capital city,
or so he likes to think . . .

CONTENTS

Foreword   5

Introduction   7

1. Dockland Scenes   9

2. Visiting Vessels   25

3. Bulldozed Butetown   43

4. Carnival Capers   63

5. Trade & Industry   73

6. Wartime Activity   125

7. Memorable Moments   137

8. Lost Landmarks   149

Postscript   159

Acknowledgements   160

FOREWORD

I'm heading down Bute Street and it's not what it was, in fact it is nothing like it was: no Charleston Club snuck by the bridge; no junction canal; no Custom House or Quebec; no flurry of shops and cafés and places with smoke and dirt coming out of them; no cladding to the Taff Vale Railway Bute Road Station embankment, the 'Welcome to Tropical Wales' slogan hacked and lost; no North Star Club, last haunt of the paralytic; no dock gates; no West Dock; no cranes; no staithes; no railtracks embedded in the roads; no steam; no saddle tankers; no whistles; no trucks of coal; no canal; no sails of ships; no flags and rigging; no huge post office; no Philanderer Club; no Dowlais; no one selling things in the street; no one dressed in worn-out working clothes and flat cap, with their pants held up by rope. The singing, the joy, the community, the dirty dark, the steam and the shouting, the bustle and the money and the smell of the sea: gone.

Cardiff's Docklands have vanished. It's hard to believe that when at its height this place was one of the world's largest industrial ports, a Saudi Arabia of dark dust and black gold, sending steam anthracite and iron and steel to the four corners of a globe that could not manage without them. Around Cardiff's five vast docks had grown a whole empire of warehouses, dry docks, storage yards, custom house, processing plant, railyards, sheds, coal staithes, tenements, boarding houses, mission, church, mosque, cafés, pubs, clubs and police station.

By the 1960s the world had moved. Who needed dirty coal when we can have clean oil? The Ferry Road Subway closed, the pumps froze and cracked at Penarth Dock, the West Dock was abandoned, shipping companies closed, warehouses stayed empty. Grass began to grow between the tracks. The canal was drained. The 150-year boom was over.

By the end of the 1980s change was in command again, rebuilding and reinventing. With a controversial stroke of unexpected and enlightened genius Cardiff had decided to redevelop itself as a waterfront leisure resort, mixing capital culture – St David's five-star hotel, the National Assembly, the Wales Millennium Centre – with apartment-led property development. Flats can sell for more if you can see the sea from their windows. Another boom slowly began and if you cross the Bay today you can see it, like a Spanish holiday resort, exploding all around you.

The old has been swept away and replaced with clean, clear concrete, steel, glass, aluminium and blond wood. Where the West Dock once took ships from the world over there are now apartments, red brick, the dock feeder realigned to make this Cardiff's Venice. Where the canal from distant Merthyr once expanded into a sea dock there is now a park. Where timber floated there are houses. Where the rail tracks became sidings stands the National Assembly's parliament house, the Senedd. Where the rough pubs threw seamen into the night, younger clubbers now track the Bay's million bars. Restaurants seethe like the floors of stock exchanges. This place has been completely reinvented. Its population displaced and disinherited. Its enterprise dulled and changed.

Its magnates moved on to other places and other businesses. Heavy industry has left us. They dig coal in Poland. They make steel in China. Round here we drink latte watching the pleasure yachts cross a freshwater, barrage-enclosed lake. There is a tourist road train that toots. There are galleries.

Bay of Tigers no longer. The Portuguese who once sailed here, eyeing the towers of Guests Glassworks to set their bearings, churning through our immense Bristol Channel tidal rise and fall, go elsewhere if they go anywhere at all.

How much of what was should we keep? Russell Goodway, former leader of the Council and Lord Mayor, wanted the canal back, but it was too late. There are a few bollards in the tarmac in the park. Along Lloyd George Boulevard are remnants of the cranes that once worked here. The Norwegian Church has been knocked down, moved and re-erected – new roof, new walls, new floor. The Pilot House was put on a lorry and moved 500m and has had a pub six times its size built onto the back. The wood-supported signals which once guided in the steamers are still there off Pierhead, and that magnificent building itself remains, tastefully refurbished and used by the Welsh Assembly as an interpretation centre. Its clock appears nightly on the Welsh television news like Big Ben. Towards Atlantic Wharf stone warehouses have been turned into gardenless apartments. There was another warehouse along Lloyd George, but that got pulled down. The Taff Vale Bute Road Station is now Arriva's Cardiff Bay – same place, more or less, but for how long?

Brian Lee's terrific collection of unearthed Docklands memories shows a lot of what could have been refurbished and reused. Things bulldozed flat in a fit of planning vandalism or maybe simply removed at speed to ensure that change would come. It is easy to forget, too, that after coal had finished Cardiff continued as an important port. Brian's photographs show the city's mid-twentieth century trade in cattle, horses, oil, eggs, timber, iron ore, fruit, crushed bones. The book's strength is in its breadth of detail: great aerial shots of what was, vast panoramas of vanished docklands, close-ups of lock gates and pub frontages, pictures of arriving ships, of dignified visitors, the Big Windsor, George Street full of Ford Cortinas, kids pulling their socks up, Loudoun Square being knocked down.

As I write, I'm at the bottom of Bute Street in sight of the freshwater sea, surrounded by new-build stores, Tesco, a tapas bar, the Comedy Club. People in soft shoes drift by, kids with ice creams, girls talking on their mobile phones. Someone should be shooting all this. It will make a fine future volume for Sutton Publishing, fifty years down the line.

Peter Finch,
Cardiff, 2006

INTRODUCTION

In the early nineteenth century Cardiff was a small town, but its proximity to the sea and its natural harbour made it an ideal site for the development of a port to serve the rapidly growing trade in coal and iron. The building of the docks during the 1830s attracted many migrant workers to the area. By the late 1890s Cardiff was Britain's largest coal-exporting port and on the eve of the First World War coal exports had reached a peak of 13 million tons.

The decline of the coal and iron industries during the 1960s and 1970s sounded the death knell for Cardiff's docklands and by the late 1980s the area had become a scene of dereliction and wasteland. It is hard to believe that today, some twenty or so years later, the area is now home to the National Assembly of Wales, the Wales Millennium Centre, the Glamorgan County Offices, thousands of new houses and apartments, cinemas, cafés, shops, commercial buildings and much, much more, providing work and pleasure for a large number of people. With the promise of exciting things to come it is possible to say that, just like the phoenix that rose from the ashes, Cardiff Docks has transformed itself.

For those people who only know the area today by its new name, Cardiff Bay, the selection of aerial views of the docks in Chapter One, 'Dockland Scenes', will surely fascinate. Tommy 'The Fish' Letton, one of Cardiff Dockland's great characters, after whom a street was named, is also recalled in this chapter, as are the long-gone cattle auctions and the Mount Stuart Dry Dock.

Chapter Two, 'Visiting Vessels', provides a glimpse of the many ships that have berthed in Cardiff over the years and the tugs, such as *Lowgarth* and *Moray Firth*, which guided them into port. Also featured is *Alexander T. Wood*, which in 1962 discharged the largest cargo of iron ore ever at the port.

We have the *Western Mail*'s magnificent picture archive to thank for Chapter Three, 'Bulldozed Butetown', which records the demolishing of not only hundreds of dilapidated terraced houses, but also of a community that was then forced to live in high-rise flats. How ironic that luxury flats, which few people can afford, are sprouting up all over the place today.

Chapter Four, 'Carnival Capers', captures the faces of the local inhabitants enjoying themselves at the annual Butetown Carnival. Sadly, I was not able to find a photograph in the newspaper's archives of me running in the Butetown Mile!

The images in Chapter Five, 'Trade & Industry', remind us of the great port Cardiff once was, and include a photograph of the *Columbialand* – the widest ship ever to enter Cardiff – on her maiden voyage from western Canada with a cargo of packaged timber. There is a picture of *Cape Nelson*, a 12,351-ton ore-carrier and one of the biggest ships to berth at Cardiff Dry Docks for repairs in 1967. Some Cardiffians may even recognise their fathers or grandfathers among the many dock workers who appear in these pages.

In Chapter Six, 'Wartime Activity', we are reminded of the great part the USA played in the Second World War. We see General Lee – no relation of the author as far as

I know – talking to dock workers and addressing them at a meeting. There is also a picture of GIs boarding the SS *Santa Paula*, one of the most active transport ships during the war.

Happier times such as royal visits, the opening of Fletchers Wharf in 1966 and the visits of nuclear submarines HMS *Warspite* and HMS *Valiant* are recorded in Chapter Seven, 'Memorable Moments'. The ill-fated Antarctic Expedition of Captain Scott in June 1910 is also remembered.

In the final chapter, 'Lost Landmarks', we revisit long-gone public houses, such as The Crown, Pembroke Castle, The Custom House and the Big Windsor (now an Indian restaurant) and relive the time when it was possible to take a trip on the festival ship *Campania* or walk down James Street in the days when Coal was King.

The images in this book come from several sources, with the chief contributors being Associated British Ports, Cardiff Council and the Western Mail & Echo Ltd.

1

Dockland Scenes

The Pierhead Building, designed by William Frame in French Gothic style, was erected in 1896. Cardiff has a rich and varied history – in Elizabethan times it was notorious as a haunt of pirates. (*Raphael Tuck & Sons*)

Derelict Ship Lane, which runs behind a row of older buildings on the west side of Bute Street, November 1976. (*Western Mail & Echo*)

Sailing ships in Roath Basin, Bute Docks. When the Roath Basin was opened in 1874, the population of Cardiff was 64,044. Before the development of the iron and coal trade, wool was the main export from Cardiff Docks. (*Viner & Co.*)

Cardiff photographer *Ernest T. Bush* took this general view of the docks in about 1894. The town had been a sea port since ancient times, but there is written evidence of its existence as a port at the end of the thirteenth century. In the *Calendar of the Close Rolls for the Reign of Edward I*, 1296–1302 it was recorded on 11 April 1300 that an order was issued to the bailiffs of Cardiff and sixty-two other ports not to permit the export of silver money without the King's special licence.

The lock dates at Bute Dock, *c.* 1900. Bute West Dock opened in October 1839 and the first part of Bute East Dock in July 1855. The second part was opened in August 1859. (*Viner & Co*)

Cardiff's biggest dock, the Queen Alexandra, *c.* 1920. The dock opened in July 1907, by which time the population of Cardiff was 182,700. At one time Cardiff was noted for the manufacture of ordnance and some local iron founders were suspected of sending supplies to Spain. A customs record for 1778 gives Richard Crawshay permission to ship 1,400 guns at Cardiff. (*New Series*)

Embedded in the terracotta tilework of the Pierhead Building – the offices of the Bute Docks Company when this picture was taken *c.* 1915 – is the motto TRWY DDWR A THAN (By Water and Fire). In 1881 the number of steamships exceeded the number of sailing ships in Cardiff for the first time. (*Western Mail & Echo*)

P. & A. Campbell pleasure steamers, *c.* 1900. They sailed from the Pierhead Building between 1886 and 1972 before moving to their current berth at Penwith. On 25 August 1887 the *South Wales Daily News* carried an advertisement for a 'Marine Excursion from Cardiff to Ilfracombe by the New Clyde-built Royal Mail Saloon Steamer *Waverley*, the greyhound of the Bristol Channel (weather and circumstances permitting)'. The return fares were 5*s* or 3*s* 6*d*, and there was a band and refreshments on board. (*Ernest T. Bush*)

Tommy Letton, *c.* 1950. He sold fish from his barrow in Butetown for more than forty years. He also found time to teach youngsters football and formed his own youth club. Letton lived in Clarence Embankment. After he died a street was named after him. (*Western Mail & Echo*)

A tram shuffles past the Clarence Road railway station, *c.* 1938. 'For just a penny the number six would take you to Llandaff Fields,' recalled former Cardiff Lord Mayor *John Smith*. Electric trams ran in Cardiff from 1902 until 1950. (*John Smith*)

Aerial view showing the mechanised timber-handling wharf at Roath Dock, 1967. Timber imports to the docks are said to date from 1813 or even earlier.

This was how Cardiff Docks looked from the air in 1958. Goods were transported by rail to the sidings (centre). Before the construction of the railways the Glamorgan Canal, built in 1794, was used to carry coal to the docks; originally coal had been brought down from the valleys on the backs of mules.

Opposite top: P. & A. Campbell pleasure steamers, seen on the right *c*. 1960, have operated in the Bristol Channel for more than a century. In the days before modern communications ships' crews would exchange news when they docked. This was how, on 11 May 1887, when the Glasgow barque *Willowbank* sailed into Falmouth she was able to report that on 25 March she had spoken to the *Occidental* (Cardiff to Acapulco, Mexico) and had heard that there had been a mutiny aboard in which the captain had been murdered by a crew member. (*Ernest T. Bush*)

Opposite bottom: Channel Dry Dock and Pontoon *c*. 1960. At one time, when there were about twelve dry docks, including Mount Stuart, Baileys, Hills and Commercial, thousands of men were employed in the area. (*Western Mail & Echo*)

Above and right: Floating cranes in action in the days when Cardiff Docks was a thriving sea port. There were 120 shipping companies operating in Cardiff in 1920.

Opposite top: Spillers Mill, Roath Dock, known to many dockers as 'The Cathedral of the Docks', c. 1950. Demolition of the building was halted in 2003 owing to the discovery of a protected species of bird that was nesting in the tower.

Opposite bottom: The new tanker-cleaning plant at Mount Stuart Dry Dock, c. 1960. In 1875 an oil-carrying vessel built in Mill Lane Foundry was launched in the Glamorgan Canal just below the old Custom House Bridge. Spectators cheered the workmen as she was hauled along skids over the bridge.

Opposite top and bottom: Cardiff Docks, *c.* 1930, was one of the few ports licensed to import live animals and was equipped with stables, lairs, an abattoir and auction rings.

A blot on the landscape: Gulf Oil tanks *c.* 1960.

The cattle lairs, Roath Dock, May 1947. Before restrictions were imposed on the importation of foreign cattle animals were landed at the docks and driven along Bute Road.

The first shipment of cattle from Canada by the Canadian Trade Corporation after the lifting of the trade embargo in 1928. An auction of the first animal ashore raised £570 for the Cardiff Royal Infirmary.

This greyhound arrived from Ireland, *c.* 1930, but whether it is the legendary Mick The Miller, as was suggested, is another matter. For the record, Mick The Miller won the 1930 Welsh Greyhound Derby at Cardiff's Welsh White City Stadium in Sloper Road.

2

Visiting Vessels

On a winter's day butter and cheese is dispatched from *Brisbane Star* straight into the
sheds at Cardiff Docks, *c.* 1950.

The *Cerro Bolivar* discharging its cargo of iron ore, July 1961. More than 800,000 tons of iron ore were imported through Cardiff to provide raw material for Dowlais Steelworks in 1900.

Right: The first cargo of crushed bones from Pakistan was discharged from the SS *Empire Spartan* at the Queen Alexandra Dock in August 1948. The bones were used to make fertiliser.

Opposite: *River Afton* docked alongside the kangaroo cranes and ore conveyor system in Roath Dock, *c.* 1960. When Roath Dock was opened in 1887 there were 115,000 people living in Cardiff.

The *Mercantile Pioneer*, *c.* 1960, made an imposing sight, as did many of the vessels which docked at Cardiff over the years. In August 1902 hundreds of people flocked to Cardiff Docks to see the arrival of two Japanese warships, *Takasago* and *Asama*. The officers and crew of the two ships totalled more than 900. Commander W. Yoshimatsu and Rear Admiral Ijoin were welcomed by the Mayor at a garden party in Sophia Gardens.

Opposite top: The *Belgulf Progress*, *c.* 1955, was one of the hundreds of oil tankers to visit Cardiff Docks. The Spillers Mill building is in the background.

Opposite bottom: Sitting at the tanker-cleaning berth at Roath Dock is the *Naranio, c.* 1950.

Not a soul in sight as the *Lucellum* awaits attention, *c.* 1960.

The smart-looking tanker *Laristan* berthed at the Roath Dock, *c.* 1950. It ran aground at Tiree in 1942 and was refloated.

Opposite top: *City of Poona* discharges crushed bones to road and rail vehicles and meat to the *Sprayville*, October 1960.

Opposite bottom: *Jalazad* brought her cargo of crushed bones to Cardiff in July 1961.

Iron ore is discharged from the *Aldersgate* by kangaroo cranes at the Guest Keen Iron and Steel wharf, *c.* 1960. With the closure of the British Steel Corporation in 1978, iron ore ceased to be imported. Left of picture is the *Waipura*.

Newcastle Star arrives in Cardiff with a cargo of refrigerated meat, February 1962. This 8,398-ton vessel was built in West Germany in 1956 and broken up in Taiwan in 1980.

Methane Pioneer, an old US Navy vessel, was replaced by *Methane Princess*. Penarth Head can be seen in the background, *c.* 1960.

British Yeoman, c. 1956, a 9,000-ton Doxford diesel tanker.

Alexander T. Wood discharged the largest cargo of iron ore, some 13,500 tons, at the port, February 1962.

Bergechief on a visit to Cardiff Docks in 1960.

Opposite top: *Cumberland* enters Queen Alexandra Dock, June 1949.

Opposite bottom: A cargo of crushed bones is discharged from *Jaljawahar*, August 1956.

Evina, built at Newcastle-on-Tyne in 1930, is berthed at Roath Dock, September 1949. By 1850, 40 per cent of the UK's iron output was being produced in South Wales.

Texaco Gloucester regularly sailed between Cardiff and Milford Haven in the 1960s with a cargo of fuel oil.

Opposite top: *Port Auckland* came to Cardiff Docks with a cargo of meat and dairy produce, September 1960.

Opposite bottom: Seen alongside *Hinakura* is the 567-ton steam coaster *Moray Firth*, 1954. Owned by G.T. Gillie, *Moray Firth* was bought by the Aberdeen Coal & Shipping Company in 1959 and was broken up at Dunstan in March 1972.

Annuity was owned by Fred Everard, a long-established shipping company.

Bunga Angsana was one of
many ships lying idle after
a strike by 260 Cardiff dock
workers in 1977. The dispute
concerned haulage facilities for
moving cargo from the port.
(*Western Mail & Echo*)

The diesel-powered tug *Lowgarth*, built in 1965, gives *Axina* a helping hand, *c.* 1970. A mission was provided for the Cardiff seafaring community in 1863 when the thirty-nine-year-old frigate HMS *Thisbe* was, at the request of the Marquess of Bute, loaned by the Admiralty. The ship was positioned first at East Bute Dock and later at the entrance of West Bute Dock. Its gun deck was fitted out as an institute and church.

Frozen meat being unloaded from *Golden Ocean* at Kings Wharf cold stores, June 1948. One of the many ships which sailed into Cardiff docks ended its days as an industrial school: the 42-gun frigate HMS *Havannah* entered East Bute Dock in 1860. Later it transferred to a more permanent berth on the side of Penarth Road, near Penarth Bridge, and was converted into the Cardiff Ragged School. In 1905 it was declared a 'decaying hulk' and was broken up after being sold for £1,030.

3

Bulldozed Butetown

Cardiff Docks and Butetown. The West Dock on the left had been filled in by the time
this picture was taken in 1969. There have been many explanations as to how the
Butetown area became known as Tiger Bay. One is that in about 1871 the singer
Harry Moreton sang a song entitled 'Tiger Bay' which mentioned Butetown.
(*Western Mail & Echo* Ltd)

Yvonne Evans and her children, Janet, 3, Stephen, 2, and Phillip, 3 months, pose for the photographer outside their condemned house on Bute Street, August 1969. (*Western Mail & Echo*)

Prize-winning photographer Alan Grist took this picture of Bute Street being dug up for resurfacing, 1964. (*Alan Grist, Western Mail & Echo*)

Under Starter's Orders! Punters try their luck in Abraham's betting shop, 1975. (*Western Mail & Echo*)

Businesses along Bute Street included Abraham's betting shop, centre, September 1968. (*Western Mail & Echo*)

Mary Newman, whose family had lived in the docks area for a century, was one of the last residents of South Church Street before the houses were demolished, 1968. (*Western Mail & Echo*)

Bute Street, showing Elliot Wire Rope works, left, which closed in the 1960s. The white-washed cottage, centre, was said to have been a parachute factory and was owned by Kenneth Davies of Cambrian Airways. (*Western Mail & Echo*)

Opposite: A bird's eye view of the new Bute Street shopping centre being built in 1969 in Tiger Bay. 'Tiger Bayee, Tiger Bayee, it's not very far from the docks. Once you get to Loudoun Square take the first turning there, Tiger Bayee, Tiger Bayee.' The song was sung to the tune of 'Goodbyee' from *Oh! What A Lovely War*. (*Western Mail & Echo*)

A bulldozer smashes the remaining brickwork of a house in West Church Street, 1969. The houses in the background in South Church Street were demolished shortly afterwards. (*Western Mail & Echo*)

Another house in West Church Street bites the dust, January 1969. (*Western Mail & Echo*)

Opposite top: Michael Johnson outside his house in South William Street, Butetown, shortly before it was demolished, *c.* 1970. He had lived here for thirty years. (*Western Mail & Echo*)

Opposite bottom: Many Cardiffians will remember Andros Ship Stores in South William Street, March 1969. (*Western Mail & Echo*)

Left to right: Irene Trottman, Gina Norman and Julie Campbell, residents of Georgina Street, August 1967. (*Western Mail & Echo*)

Opposite top: The former London, Midland and Scottish warehouse, a listed building in Atlantic Wharf, was converted into an attractive upmarket hotel in the 1990s. (*Western Mail & Echo*)

Opposite bottom: Collingdon Road lies derelict and deserted, January 1969. The street was named after Thomas Collingdon, secretary to the Bute Trustees. (*Western Mail & Echo*)

Left: Richard Batten's butcher's shop stood on the corner of Bute Street and Crichton Street. Mr Batten, right, with his wife and daughter, show off the Christmas fare in 1896. (*Western Mail & Echo*)

Opposite: Bute Avenue showing the Crown on the left of the road and The Custom House on the right, September 1995. (*Western Mail & Echo*)

Below: Crichton Street in 1967. The Crown Inn can be seen behind the parked cars. (*Western Mail & Echo*)

A view of the Methodist Mission church, August 1964. (*Western Mail & Echo*)

The remnants of George Street, off James Street, in 1979. The building far left is the Cardiff Castle public house. (*Western Mail & Echo*)

Dockland houses before they were demolished in the 1960s. (*Western Mail & Echo*)

Opposite: 'Socks Up'. This picture won *Western Mail* trainee photographer Alan Grist, 19, first prize in the annual Cymru Deg photographic competition, November 1963. (*Western Mail & Echo*)

Above: This little boy is playing in Loudoun Square, *c.* 1960. One hundred years before the square was one of the most prestigious parts of Cardiff's docklands. (*Western Mail & Echo*)

View from the roof of a block of flats showing the Free Masons Hotel, top right, August 1964. (*Western Mail & Echo*)

Old and new stand side by side. These new blocks in Loudoun Square together contained 120 two-bedroom apartments, July 1969. (*Western Mail & Echo*)

The derelict Imperial House which stood on the corner of Adelaide Street and James Street, *c.* 1980. (*Western Mail & Echo*)

Above: The long-gone Sailors' Home in Stuart Street opened in 1856 and was financed by the Marquis of Bute. It was photographed *c*. 1900. (*Author's collection*)

Left: The Swing Bridge over the Glamorgan Canal in James Street was built in 1904. This photograph was probably taken in the 1920s. (*Author's collection*)

Opposite: Despite being surrounded by dereliction, this little boy was having a swinging time in Loudoun Square, February 1969. (*Western Mail & Echo*)

The Gospel Mission Hall in Angelina Street played a major part in the life of Butetown. The mission provided soup for down and outs. The gentleman seated in the front row is Mr Bowyer and the picture is believed to have been taken in 1939. (*Western Mail & Echo*)

'On the Move!' A resident of Angelina Street moves some of his belongings to his new flat, *c.* 1975. (*Western Mail & Echo*)

4

Carnival Capers

Liana Farrah, 4, and Karime Hassan, 7, who were chosen as Fairy Queen and Prince
Charming for the Mardi Gras at the Butetown Community Centre, 1969.
(*Western Mail & Echo*)

A bird's eye view of some of the 40,000 people who attended the Butetown Carnival held in August 1985. (*Western Mail & Echo*)

'Now you see it. Now you don't.' Cardiff magician Eric Black entertaining the crowd at the 1985 Butetown Carnival. (*Western Mail & Echo*)

'Beat out that rhythm on a drum!' Pat Howell (left) of Miskin Street, Cathays, Cardiff, and Sheila Evelyn of Newborough Avenue, Llanishen, Cardiff, enjoying themselves at the 1985 Butetown Carnival. (*Western Mail & Echo*)

Above: *Echo* photographer David Evans took this delightful picture of 4-year-old Bethan Bruford and her 6-year-old brother Geraint at the 1985 Butetown Carnival. (*Western Mail & Echo*)

Opposite: Twelve-year-old Kevin Khan of Christina Street, Butetown, looks at the mural on a wall along Bute Street, 1983. (*Western Mail & Echo*)

Right: No doubt the young girl, left, grew up to be a ballet dancer! Butetown Carnival 1986. (*Western Mail & Echo*)

Below: Members of a large crowd enjoying the Bank Holiday sunshine and music as they listen to Aswad, Avanti and other big bands at the 1987 Butetown Carnival. (*Western Mail & Echo*)

It was all swings and roundabouts for these youngsters at the 1988 Butetown Carnival. (*Western Mail & Echo*)

Below: Tiger Bay's Arab population celebrates a religious festival in the 1950s. (*Western Mail & Echo*)

Opposite: Members of the Butetown Youth Centre make their way along Bute Street during the Butetown Carnival parade, 1988. (*Western Mail & Echo*)

'Dancing The Night Away!' The 1990 Butetown Carnival festivities continued well into the evening with a full programme of live groups and entertainment. (*Western Mail & Echo*)

5

Trade & Industry

The new sheds at Queen Alexandra Dock, 1972. The dock was opened by King
Edward VII in 1907. (*Western Mail & Echo*)

Raw sugar from SS *Baron Ramsay* is stacked by electric escalator at A Shed, Queen Alexandra Dock, May 1949.

Raw sugar stored in A Shed, Queen Alexandra Dock, May 1949.

The 12,351-ton ore-carrier *Cape Nelson* awaits repairs in the dry dock, May 1967. (*Western Mail & Echo*)

Above: Sacks of
crushed bones are
discharged to road
vehicles, February
1962.

Right: Dock workers
unload a cargo of
oranges to road
vehicles, *c*. 1960.

Opposite: Dock
workers discharge
general cargo
to road and rail
transport, *c*. 1960.

A cargo of bananas is loaded onto road vehicles, 1957.

Sacks of potatoes being discharged at Queens Dock, June 1947.

Cargo from Canada arrives at Kings Wharf, August 1946.

Boxes of 'Veri Best' tomatoes from Cilicia are stacked in A Shed, April 1950.

Opposite top: Dockers unload sacks of potatoes to Coastal Roadways vehicles, *c*. 1960.

Opposite bottom: Sugar being stored in A Shed, Queen Alexandra Dock, May 1949.

Right and below: Some of the 2,200 cars waiting to be loaded onto ships for export to America, July 1968. Cardiff Docks enjoyed a minor boom in the 1960s thanks to a sudden upturn in the car export trade. (*Western Mail & Echo*)

'Gently Does It!' Cargo is stacked into railway carriages, *c.* 1960.

Opposite top: Frozen meat is discharged from the SS *Deseado* to Kings Wharf, *c.* 1960.

Opposite bottom: Dockers receive imported frozen meat at the New Cold Store, 1949.

Above and below: Landing slings of frozen meat onto the apron at Kings Wharf Cold Store, 1969.

Opposite top and bottom: Dockers unload frozen meat from the SS *Arawa* at Kings Wharf Cold Store in the 1960s.

A cargo of 8,800 tons of
Canadian flour is unloaded
from the SS *Seaside* in
August 1946.

Dockers stack bags of sugar at A Warehouse, August 1945.

Opposite top: Dockers in the hold of the SS *Empire Spartan* discharge a cargo of crushed bones from Pakistan, Queen Alexandra Dock, August 1948.

Opposite bottom: Just some of the thousands of sacks of grain stacked in B Shed, June 1950.

The storage tanks of the Regent Oil Company, *c.* 1960. Penarth Head is in the background, top right. (*Western Mail & Echo*)

An engineer checks the fans as they blow air into the £20,000 inflatable transit shed on the quay at the Queens Dock, April 1971. The 260ft-long by 60ft-high transit shed was used to increase the tonnage of fruit coming to the port. (*Western Mail & Echo*)

In the 1950s Guest Keen and Baldwin operated an oil pipeline at Roath Dock. Today Fuel and Marine Marketing runs a heavy-fuel-oil and distribution terminal at Cardiff Docks.

The *Belgulf Progress* berthed at Cardiff Docks, *c.* 1970. A 4,000-ton oil depot was built at Queen Alexandra Dock in 1933 to enable bulk supplies to be imported by direct shipment from overseas.

'All hands to deck.' These dock workers have an audience, *c.* 1960.

The *Mercantile Pioneer, c.* 1960. Today Cardiff Docks offers a petrol and diesel distribution facility operated by Simon Storage on behalf of Chevron Texaco.

The new Spillers & Bakers Mill was built in 1936 and manufactured ship biscuits, dog biscuits and poultry foods.

For many years Cardiff Docks has been dealing in liquid bulks from chemicals, petrochemicals, fuel and diesel oil. This photograph was taken *c.* 1960.

Opposite: The docks at Cardiff were one of the few licensed to import live cattle, *c.* 1950. As long ago as 1891, 1,600 heads of cattle were imported from Chicago.

Cattle are sorted out by their handlers, *c.* 1930.

Opposite top and bottom: Canadian cattle are unloaded at Roath Dock, 1928.

Army horses from the USA were among the livestock imported through the docks, *c.* 1945.

Opposite top and bottom: Dutch cattle leaving SS *Orestes* at Roath Dock, October 1947.

Dock workers watch the tug *Uskgarth* towing a ship alongside the swing bridge at the Queen Alexandra Dock. The *Uskgarth* was built in 1966.

Rapier mobile crane in action at Queen Alexandra Dock, *c.* 1960.

Eggs from Canada are loaded onto road vehicles at Queen Alexandra Dock, November 1948.

'Where do you want this lot, boss?' *c.* 1960.

Over the years various kinds of vehicles for shifting materials at the docks have been used as these two photographs illustrate (above, *c.* 1950; below, *c.* 1960).

Cases of French brandy are unloaded in time for the 1963 Christmas market. Before the docks were built this was a perilous coast for shipping. In 1712 a French vessel laden with wine and brandy ran ashore at Sully, just along the coast from Cardiff, and her cargo was seized by custom officers. Locals armed with guns and pistols tried to steal the brandy. But Mr Morgan, the Comptroller of Cardiff, and his officers, assisted by local residents, were able to disperse the mob. (*Western Mail & Echo*)

Aerial view of Cardiff Docks, *c.* 1950, once the premier port in the United Kingdom.

Above: Meat and dairy produce from New Zealand is unloaded onto British Road Services vehicles, Queen Alexandra Dock, September 1960.

Vehicles belonging to Noah Rees & Griffiths are stacked with hay from Norway, 1950.

Unloading hay from Norway, 1950.

Above: A cargo of 7,500 standards of packaged timber, about 25,000 tons, being discharged from *Columbialand* at the new berth at Queen Alexandra Dock, *c.* 1968. The ship was on her maiden voyage from Western Canada and was the widest ship to enter Cardiff. (*Western Mail & Echo*)

Opposite top: In 1970 Cardiff dockers set a new record when they discharged more than 10.5 million board feet of packaged timber from the motor ship *Vancouver Forest* pictured here. The ship was one of eight similar vessels equipped with Hagglund electro-hydraulic deck cranes. (*Western Mail & Echo*)

Opposite bottom: A cargo of 2,500 tons of timber is unloaded from three Polish ships at Fletcher Wharf, 1966. (*Western Mail & Echo*)

Above: Goods are transported onwards by road and rail, *c.* 1960.

Right: Dairy produce from New Zealand is unloaded, May 1969.

Opposite top: Dockers discharge timber from a bulk timber carrier, 1977.

Opposite bottom: Timber is unloaded at Fletchers Wharf using mechanical handling appliances, *c.* 1970.

Goods from New Zealand are discharged by means of a roller runway in the hold of a ship, *c.* 1960.

Opposite top: Frozen meat is brought ashore from the SS *Unmaston Grange*, 1949.

Opposite bottom: Unloading New Zealand frozen meat, 1961.

Above: Frozen meat is unloaded, 1960.

Left: A cargo of frozen meat from Australia is stacked onto a wagon, *c.* 1960.

Opposite top: Boxes of oranges are loaded onto British Road Services vehicles, *c.* 1960.

Opposite bottom: A forklift driver stacks palleted fruit in the sheds, *c.* 1960.

Above and right: The year is 1947 and iron ore was still being landed at the docks.

Opposite: Boxed goods from New Zealand are loaded onto road and rail vehicles at Kings Wharf, September 1960.

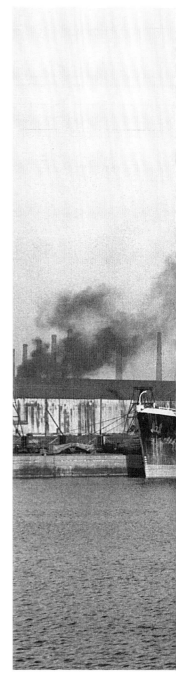

Above: *Oredian* discharges iron ore at Guest Keen Iron & Steel Company's new kangaroo iron-ore berth, *c*. 1960.

Opposite top: The Mount Stuart oil-tanker cleaning installation, Roath Dock, 1959.

Opposite centre: Cattle lairs at Roath Dock, *c*. 1950.

Opposite bottom: A Simson floating crane in action, *c*. 1960.

Perishable goods are discharged from the SS *Wairangi* to Kings Wharf Cold Stores, April 1947. The ship was built in 1942 and named *Empire Grace*; it was scrapped in 1963.

Work is under way to fill in Bute Dock Basin at the entrance to the old Bute Dock, 1970.

Bute West Dock, 1962. The dock opened in October 1839 and had four hydraulic cranes for discharging timber and ballast. (*Western Mail & Echo*)

6

Wartime Activity

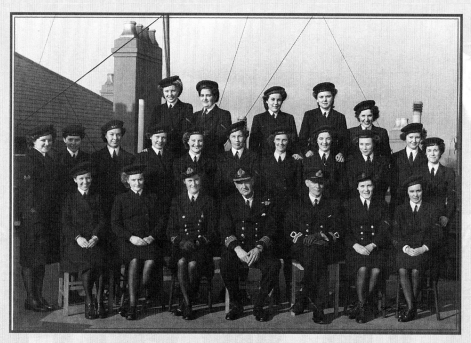

During the Second World War Imperial Building was used as the Naval base HMS *Lucifer*. This picture shows communications staff on the roof of the building in 1945.
(*Catherine Squance*)

Above: American General Lee shakes hands with dockers; *below*: General Lee addresses a meeting, 1946.

The discharge of American locomotives from the sea train *Texas*, November 1942. The crew have draped the first engine ashore with the Union Jack and the Stars and Stripes.

Vehicles being discharged from the sea train *Texas*, March 1944.

Above: A Centurion tank is unloaded at Roath Dock in the early 1950s.

Left: A tank is discharged from a Landing Ship (Tank) vessel, 1944.

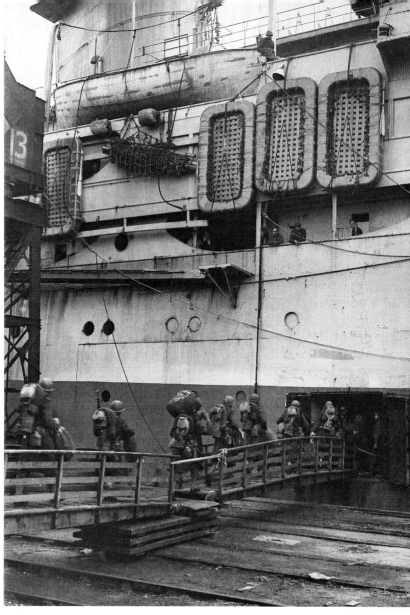

Above right: In 1943 American troops board the SS *Santa Paula*, one of the most active transport ships of the Second World War. Built in 1932, she could hold more than 2,200 passengers and in four years made twenty-eight overseas voyages.

Right: General cargo from the USA, including foodstuffs, is unloaded from the SS *Inishowen Head*, 1946.

Women at work in the docks while the men were at war, *c.* 1943.

During an air raid in 1941 the Crown Fuel Company was put out of action.

Tank landing craft are
discharged by floating
crane during the Second
World War.

A Jeep is hoisted on a
60-ton self-propelled floating
crane, October 1943.

Cardiff Docks Auxiliary Firefighters line up for a group photograph, February 1944. Cardiff Docks had its own firefighters as the port was considered to be at high risk from enemy bombers during the Second World War.

Home Guard and Civil Defence parade, 1943.

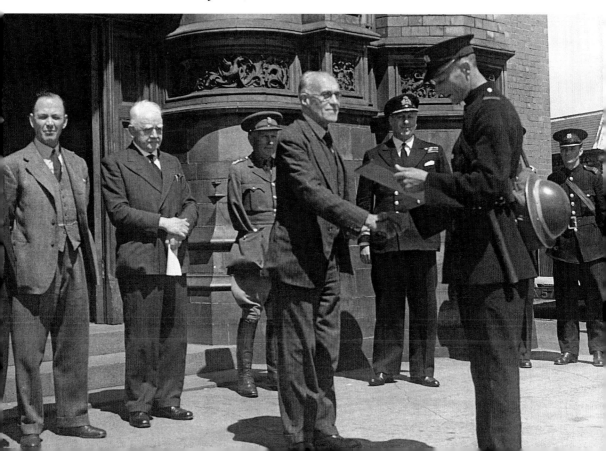

The hospital ship *Atlantis* berthed in the Queen Alexandra Dock, July 1943. Note the barrage balloon.

SS *Largo Bay* berthed at Cardiff Docks.

7

Memorable Moments

Capt Robert Falcon Scott and his gallant crew sailed from Cardiff Docks on the
SS *Terra Nova* on 15 June 1910 on their ill-fated expedition to the South Pole.
(*Author's collection*)

As part of the Festival of Britain celebrations, HMS *Campania* visited Cardiff from 31 July to 11 August 1951. The former aircraft carrier was used as a floating exhibition ship and during its stay in the Queen Alexandra Dock was visited by 104,391 people. Originally built in 1943 as a refrigerated freighter, *Campania* took part in the atomic bomb trials on Monte Bello Island in the South Pacific on 3 October 1952.

HMS *Diadem* visited Cardiff Docks in October 1949. (*Cardiff Central Library*)

King George VI and
Queen Elizabeth,
accompanied by
Princess Elizabeth, on a
visit to Cardiff, March
1941. During the tour
they inspected the local
Civil Defence units.

Civic dignitaries await the royal party on the occasion of the Prince of Wales's investiture in 1969. Sixth from the left is James Callaghan, MP for Cardiff South-East and Penarth and Prime Minister 1976–9.

Opposite: The Lord Mayor of Cardiff, Alderman Ferguson Jones, on a visit to Cardiff Docks, December 1978.

Guests at the opening of Fletchers Wharf, Roath Dock, 1966. (*Western Mail & Echo*)

Opposite top: British Transport Docks Board float at the 1968 Lord Mayor's Parade.

Opposite bottom: The captain of HMS *Cambrian* welcomes aboard an important visitor, *c.* 1970.

PROGRESS AND DEVELOPMENT

CARDIFF DOCKS

SYDNEY
MELBOURNE
WELLINGTON
PERSIAN GULF
PORT SAID

NEW YORK
HAMBURG
COPENHAGEN
CAPE TOWN
TOULOUSE

GATEWAY TO THE WORLD

AMBRIAN

Above and opposite: HMS *Warspite*, a sister ship to the nuclear submarine HMS *Valiant* (opposite), both of which docked at Cardiff in 1977. (*Cardiff Central Library*)

Right: Marconi Maritime wireless driver tests the Marconi telegraphic equipment aboard the *African Prince*, 1951.

The Royal family say their farewells before boarding the Royal Yacht *Britannia* after their visit to Wales in June 1965.

On another Royal visit
to Wales the Queen
and Duke of Edinburgh
take their leave of the
hundreds of people
who gathered at the
docks to see them off,
1969.

The Royal Yacht *Britannia* brought Prince Charles to Wales in 1969, the year of his investiture. The 3,990-ton ship was built on the Clyde in 1953.

8

Lost Landmarks

Clarence Road Bridge was opened by the Duke of Clarence on 19 September 1890.
(*Author's collection*)

Above and opposite: James Street in the days when Coal was King, *c.* 1920. (*Cardiff Central Library*)

Eleanor Street was ready for demolition when this picture was taken in 1962. (*Cardiff Central Library*)

Christina Street, 1965, with the new tower blocks of Tiger Bay in the distance. (*Cardiff Central Library*)

The Anglesey Arms Tavern in Bute Street was established at about the same time as the Pembroke Castle (*see* page 155) in the late nineteenth century. (*Cardiff Central Library*)

The Big Windsor, established in 1855 and shown here in 1988, was well-known for its gastronomic delights and was visited by many famous people, including authors Gwyn Thomas, Daniel Farson and Henry Williamson and film actors Katharine Hepburn, Kenneth More, Hugh Griffith and Noël Coward. It is now an Indian restaurant. (*Cardiff Central Library*)

Opposite: The Pembroke Castle in Louisa Street was established in 1881. (*Author's collection*)

Norwegian crews transported coal from Cardiff all over the world. The Norwegian Seamen's Mission, shown here in the 1950s, stood on the eastern side of the West Bute Dock from 1866 to 1959. It has since been replaced by a replica of the church as it was in 1889. (*Cardiff Central Library*)

Another Bute Street pub that is just a memory is The Crown. Anne Moloney was the last landlady of this popular watering hole when it was demolished in 1998. (*Cardiff Central Library*)

Left: The Custom House pub in Bute Street opened in about 1859 and became a regular haunt of the ladies of the night. It was demolished in the late 1990s. (*Cardiff Central Library*)

The fourth Marquess of Bute opened the Royal Hamadryad Seamen's Hospital in Ferry Road on 29 June 1905. It was named after a 46-gun frigate which had been used as a hospital from 1 November 1866 for sailors with infectious diseases. Voluntary contributions of 2s a ton of cargo carried by registered ships visiting the docks helped to finance the running of the hospital. It is shown here c. 1940. (*Cardiff Central Library*)

Mount Stuart Dry Dock, 1990. The dry docks had played an important role as they served the huge number of ships that arrived in ballast before loading their coal or cargo. The docks were also available for hire to enable repairs to be carried out to ships coming into the port.

POSTSCRIPT

Today Cardiff Docks may not be the port it once was, but Associated British Ports (ABP) has invested in it over the past few years and according to its handbook: 'The port has three forest-products terminals utilised by regular liner services from the Baltic states and Scandinavia.'

As for steel and other materials, the ABP handbook says: 'Cardiff is a major steel-handling port and receives shipments of steel from all over the world.' On the subject of general cargo: 'Cardiff handles a range of general and project cargoes, including coated pipes, mining supports and rail carriages, and can offer berths for heavy ro-ro activity. In 2005 a new berth was completed in Queen Alexandra Dock, to facilitate the handling of heavy-lift project cargo.' With regard to liquid bulks: 'Extensive storage and dedicated handling facilities are available for a variety of liquid-bulk cargoes.' We are also informed that: 'State-of-the-art storage and handling facilities – operated by ABP Connect – are provided for all types of fresh produce and perishables,' and that 'Cardiff Container Terminal, operated by Coastal Container Line, continues to develop new business'.

ACKNOWLEDGEMENTS

I would like to express my grateful thanks to Andrew Davies, Deborah Willcox and Pat Thompson of Cardiff Council for contacting me and asking me to compile this book and for allowing me access to the city council's archives. Also, an extra thank you to Deborah for scanning many of the photographs I selected. I would also like to thank Tony Woolway, chief librarian at Western Mail & Echo Ltd, for his help and Katrina Coopey and her staff at the Local Studies Department, Cardiff Central Library.

My special thanks go to Peter Finch, poet, author, critic and Chief Executive of the Welsh Academy, the Welsh Literature Promotion Agency and Society of Writers, for writing the foreword. Also deserving of my thanks are those people who lent me photographs. And finally, my thanks to Simon Fletcher of Sutton Publishing, who stood by me when I was going through a difficult time and who would not allow me to give up on the project.